The honey bee is one of the smallest creatures in the world, but it may be the most important for life on earth. It is the planet's greatest pollinator—moving pollen from one plant to another, causing flowers to produce seeds and fruits.

Honey bees can live in the wild or in boxes made by beekeepers. A honey bee can't live alone. It's part of a family that works closely together. A bee is always changing jobs: first she is a cleaner, then a babysitter, a builder, a guard, a scout, and finally a harvester.

This is the story of a scout. . . .

For my first grandchild, Spencer Bond
   R. H.

To Dad — a farmer who understands bees
   B. L.

First U.S. edition 2013

Library of Congress Catalog Card Number 2013931462
ISBN 978-0-7636-6760-3

TLF 18 17 16 15 14 13
10 9 8 7 6 5 4 3 2 1

Printed in Dongguan, Guangdong, China

This book was typeset in Din Schrift and Gill Sans.
The illustrations were done in watercolor, acrylic ink, and colored pencil.

Candlewick Press
99 Dover Street
Somerville, Massachusetts 02144

visit us at www.candlewick.com

Flight of the Honey Bee

RAYMOND HUBER

BRiAN LOVELOCK

CANDLEWICK PRESS

A bee the size of a cherry pit crawls from the hive. Her stripes glow golden in the morning sun. Scout has spent her whole life in the crowded hive. Now it is time for her to fly out and explore the world—time to search for flowers from which to collect pollen and nectar for food.

Her sister bees are inside, making honey, but will there be enough? The cold is coming, and Scout must find the last flowers of the fall.

There are about 50,000 female bees in a hive, and very few males.

Scout's wings hum to life,
so fast that they are almost invisible, lifting
her into the wide sky. She rises in a spiral,
up and away from the hive.

Scout remembers what she passes as
she flies, so later she can return home.

*Bees navigate using sunlight,
landmarks, and smell.
They also have a magnetic sense
that is like a built-in compass.*

Scout flies swift and straight as an arrow.
The wind buffets her, ruffling the fine hairs
on her face, but she keeps on steadily and rides
out the rapids. Eyes as black as polished stones
are searching—seeking a splash of color below.

An arresting smell drifts on the breeze.
Scout locks onto this scent.
She flies over a clearing, and spread before her
is a marvelous meadow—an ocean of flowers.

*Bees are furry,
even their eyeballs.
The hairs help them
sense changes in the wind.*

10

Bees have a powerful sense of smell.
They use their antennae to pick up scents.
Bees can smell in "stereo," each antenna
smelling in a different direction.

A flash of feathers!

A hungry blackbird swoops for the kill.
But Scout zips down and escapes into the trees,
weaving between tangled twigs.

Many creatures eat honey bees,
including other insects such as
wasps and dragonflies,
as well as spiders, frogs, birds,
and mammals such as
bears and badgers.

When the coast is clear, Scout is drawn to the sea of flowers again.
She settles on a velvety petal and plunges her head into the flower.
Here is sunken treasure: a cup of sweet nectar. The tip of her tongue,
shaped like a miniature spoon, sips the syrup.

Scout zigs and zags from flower to flower, spreading pollen around.
The pollen clings to her fuzzy body—a sprinkle of sun-powder.

Bees are charged with static electricity during flight,
which attracts pollen to their bodies.
They have an extra stomach in which they carry nectar home.

Scout has finished drinking.
She must tell her sister bees about this
field of blue. But a thundercloud cloaks
the sun. All at once, the cloud bursts.
Rain batters Scout to the ground.
She crawls under a leaf as hailstone
bombs explode around her.

Bees avoid rain and storms.
Raindrops can damage them
and chill their wing muscles,
leaving them grounded.

Wasps invade beehives to steal
honey and eat baby bees.

The downpour passes. Scout picks up the scent
of her hive and follows it.

Outside the hive, there's a squad of guard bees.
A yellow-jacketed enemy is attacking. Scout knows
that twitchy way of flying—it's a wasp!

The wasp grabs Scout as she glides in to land.
It raises its stinger, but the guards move in,
wrestling the wasp with their legs.

*Honey bees sting only
to defend themselves.
They will die after
stinging larger animals.*

Scout is safe inside the hive at last.
She begins a dance on the wax comb.
An audience gathers, captivated by the
floral scent on Scout's body.

Scout spins a story in dance,
every movement a sentence.
Scout waggles, twists, and turns,
describing the route to the blue meadow.
She pauses only to share samples
of sweet nectar.

Scout repeats her dance for many
sister bees.

The bees' dance is a complex language
that can communicate millions
of different messages.

20

Now that the sister bees know where to find the meadow, hundreds of bees take off. They flick from the hive like golden pebbles.

Bees need to harvest nectar from more than two million flowers to make enough honey to fill just one jar.

Back in the hive, Scout passes her precious nectar
to the house bees. They put it in the comb
and fan it with their wings.
The nectar will be transformed into
liquid gold—honey for the bees to eat!

*Nectar is mostly water until the bees dry
and thicken it by beating their wings,
converting it to honey.*

Scout visits the nursery, where babysitter
bees pluck the pollen from her body
and mix it with honey to feed the babies.

*The queen can lay thousands of eggs a day. It is the job of
the few male bees in the hive to fertilize a new queen.*

Nearby sits the queen, long and lustrous.
She is mother of all the bees, laying eggs
that look like tiny grains of rice.

In its lifetime, a bee can travel
more than 500 miles (800 km) on flower runs,
until its wings eventually wear out.

Exhausted after her mission, Scout rests
her silvery wings for a spell. Soon she will
join her sister bees in the blue meadow
for the fall harvest. With enough honey,
her family can now survive the winter.

Scout's daring flight has been worth every
beat of her wings.

Save the bees!

Pollination by bees gives us delicious apples, cherries, strawberries, nuts, and many vegetables. But honey bees are in danger of dying out. You can help bees by giving them food and clean places to live.

Plant a variety of flowers, herbs, and flowering trees.

Don't use toxic chemicals in gardens.

Don't pollute the air or water.

These steps will also help other pollinators, such as bumblebees, butterflies, small native bees, and other insects.

Look up the pages to find out about all these honey bee things. Don't forget to look at both kinds of words—this kind and *this kind*.

Index